THIS IS WHERE YOU CAN REACH ME NOW

Original works by: Ari Rothschild

To my loving parents and brother.

Your patience and unrelenting courage continue
to inspire me.

I love you.

I LOSE MYSELF in the wake of emotion,
words being my guardian
and the pen my sword.

I find solace in this sword,
a mighty one, sturdy
ink dribbling from the tip
as I roll it against the paper.

It reaps meaning just as it
facilitates thought, now cemented
in the cream paperback;
for the sword plunges heavily
            when
its wielder has noble cause.

TEETER OVER THE EDGE
see what you'll find
I promise it won't all be pleasant
keep in mind.
But you will see truth
that I can vouch
kindly remove your hat as you enter,
for he is no slouch.

He is kind
he is swift
his actions are a gift,
but it is your preception
that gives him his lift.

So keep believing
and you'll undoubtedly see,
a poetic genius at work
barking up the right tree.

WHEN I CLOSE MY EYES
I feel your presence
caressing the soft
silouhette swaying beneathe
my eyelids. And you
stand there looking back
at me withfierce pupils
and dancing shadows and wonder
how long it will take me
to get to you.
I stare back and think
I'm staring into your soul
but it's a mirage illuminated
by a lifetime of open-heartedness
and I melt. Not because
of your stunning beauty
but because of your auora now
gracefully lifting from
this earthly presence into
he next as it glides towards
me. And I feel you inside me warming
the very soul that youhelped me
craft but will forever
be under construction.

Together, we carry onward.

2

TAKE MY HAND
close your eyes
feel my fingers lock withyours
our soul breathes life.

The Buddha on your chest says protect me,
but i find myself feeling your comfort from afar.
Walking away fromyour sensual touch,
freed into interlocking feelings of aggression.

And I fear that our meanings get lost
in a trail of constant yearning.
Whenwhat you really want
is the grasp on an aching soul's desires.

When we walk your hand slips to my backside
and I feel your sexual energy radiating, waiting.
You want my body
I want your soul.

And I feel the separation of this world and yours.
A place of physical freedom, unlocked from the
shackles of earthly presence.
When I lift off I don't land
next to you.

When I think, I don't fear you or your thoughts
but I wonder if your energy wil be solidified
and you will finally be released from your prison.
Desires, commonwealth.

Because the spirit of the pheonix is within you
next to the cougar.
Let the pheonix fly
and accept your powerful renewal.

WHEN I MOVE MY SOUL
stays with you, for you
are my guardian angel
and protector from evil.
And I see you for you
as I see myself as a realm
of limitless possibilities.

When I imagine your mind
mine becomes a
knot, for your clutter
outweighs the most
unkind storage closet.

Peaking inside your
head might be an
EMP to my electromagnetic
brain waves and maybe
I'm being too cocky.

But my conscious is clear
and I see through your bullshit.
So open up.
Listen to me. You
might just learn how
to be free.

THE ANT came home today
to his favorite meal
of grubs and sticks.
He had moved
six rocks today
his boss was proud
his wife was proud
but something was different
it wasn't pride that warmed
his home
but a new sensation
a heat source that burned
with a furious passion
and the ant saw
a light
shine through his
rock futon
newly purchased
from Ants 'R Us
crumbled halfward
the light remaining
as an essence of solidified being
and the ant wondered
whether the light
brought a new living room
or pieces of the old
for the light had only come
today.

THE BURDEN OF THE POET

TODAY I"LL SIT HERE
with my hands in my hair
wondering just how muchof it
I'll pull out. The burden of
the poet has risen
to the surface level
and I can feel my
insides burn and bones
ache. And today I feel remorse for
sometimes I wish it was not
my burden to bare.

Sometimes I wish I
was the wind.
Only seeing and touching
the earthly obstacles
for breif moments before
continuing to be
lost in the universe.

And then I pull myself
back. Back to where
sounds break silence
and license plates
have meaning. I look
at you staring back
at me and remember,
I am the wind.

WHEN I LOSE YOUnot all of you will be gone.
I feel you hold my hand
and your spirit warms
my soul.
You're presence is
a red cherry in a bushel of dried prunes
and you're energy carries
me through the darkness.
When I am alone
I feel you touchmy cheek .
your soft hands with moisterized
calusses brush against my birthmark.
You take me home sometimes, whenI am lost.
You carry me on your shoulders when I am tired.
You give me a hanky to dry my tears on.

But you're not here.
And I'm not there.

So together we walk the earth
forever lost in a carousel
of poetic justice
and untimely presence.

THE SOULREAPS what thesoul sows
so the harvest is plentiful
for the poet.

For the poet sees
what is there
and says what needs
to be said.

And the poet
apologizes when he
shouldn't and capitalizes
on the universal
aroma of empathy.

Look at the stars
and see the poet's
playful creations
dusting into the night.

THE BOY comes home
anxious to sit in his spot
for supper
but today the fence
is off the hinge
so he pushes it open
hanging from one bolt
on top
and looks ahead
at where his home
used to be.

The boy picks up a
shard of newspaper
half burnt
November 2nd, 1971
the one mama hung
on the bulletin board
in the kitchen.

And the boy cried
because that was
last week's paper
the one that had him
on the front page
smiling
and holding his karate
medal
first prize
and mama hung his
medal over the sink.

The boy felt hands
around his shoulders
grip him tightly
it was mama
she was crying
too.

Mama did my medal
burn?
The boy cried
because she didn't ansmer
him
and the fence
fell off its hinge
accross the yard.

LET ME TAKE YOUR SOUL
for I know what to do withit.
I will caress and car for it
for it has been damaged and needs caressing.

Take my words
because they may be the most concrete ameoba
in your life right now
and make themyour own.

Feel the aches and yearns
festeing in side you
and release them
along withall of your envy.

Take time to reflect
for one day you will lookback
and wonder whyyou didn't take time
to reflect on thatwhich matters most.

Heed a warning
for warnings don't always come
in flashing neon lights.

Creativity is the basis of life
where life bleeds continuously and without . . .
interruption.

YOU'RE PRESENCE SENDS
a message and I respect
you for that. You walk
like you've got somewhere to
be and wear your
hair in careless fashion.

Yet your soul yearns for more.
You walk the earth
like it's yours when
it is ours.
Yes, we inhabit
a too large sum of
this beautiful land
we call our home.
But that doesn't mean
it shouldn't be shared
and enjoyed by the likes of
those that are already
here.

Be there.
Be here.

But where ver
you go, be present.

SUN SYMPHONY

MY HANDS sink to my waist and I know my stomach
will be quick to follow. I see the sun setting
closeto the horizon, it's irredescent glow m
melting into the thine line of darkness separatin
the sky and the water.

And I feel a hand grab mine, as if it were
bringing me back down to this earthly prescence
from the airways above.

I look to what that hand is connected to
and it's you.You're standing next to me with
a smile wider than the horizon itself.

I feel a prescence to you. As if the arth
willdrop out beneathe us and sink into its
center.

We raise into the air, meeting the sun and
shaking its hand with force but gentle
submission.

And together, me, you and the sun share a
gaze and sway lightly with the wind.

I SEE you when walk
into the room
your stare fixed
solemnly on the cocktail
in front of you.
And you fear
it's not looking back.

Your mind wanders to
the olive
tipped lazily on its side
holding onto its
firm grasp
with the toothpick
speared through its center.

And the olive becomes aware
that the toothpick
skewered baneathe its heart
and body
is the only thing connecting
its earthly presence to
the gravitational pull.

So the olive leans
as the woman sips her drink
and lipstick smears accross
the glass
before she wipes the rest off
withthe back of her hand
and takes the olive
and throws it to the ground
reminding herself
that olives
aren't alive.

Moondance Children

When the sun rises I'll be on a hill
just above a small neighboorhood soccer field
and I'll see the skydew seep into oblivion
as the sun pierces the night.

I hear the children playing in the distance
noting how early it is and considering the morning
morning mellow harshed.

And I'll watch them kick a soccer ball,
one faking the other out with his right foot
before maneuvering the ball around him with his
left.
The boys squeal with glee as the sun drift
over the horizon in seamless fashion.

I'll look up at the sky and notice the lingering
stars amongst the blue backdrop,
reluctant to go where stars go where stars go
during the day.
I wonder if the stars have families.
Do they go home for supper after a long night
of playing amongst eachother?
I picture them dance before disappearing
into the morning skyscape, retreating to
their respective homes.

The sky is an irradescent blue now and the
sunrise is complete.
I turn around to catch a glimpse of the moon
still hanging lazily above me.
The moon waves and I wave back and the
faint stars huddle in close to the moon with
his hands wrapped around their heavenly glow,
happy for them to be home.

DANCING WITH THE WIND

THE sweet tenderness of your touch
melts my fingers as they lock into yours
and I feel your heartbeat sync with mine.

Our eyesplayfully join   in lockandyour
lips curl as the spirit in the room rises.

Can you feel it? Can you feel itbeating through
your soul like a drum possessed by a lunar
diety dancing with the wind?

And I grab your hand becauseI feel that it
is the only thing keeping me grounded to this
'verse and I stop and stare and imagine a world
where it were always like this. A world where
fellow mankind walked the streets of civilization
blessed and humbled by the world that our fellow
mankind before us had created and we get to
grace its presence.

And I fear that that world is far away yet
not unreachable.
We as humans have the capacity to adapt
just as we have for thousands of years
and discover again what is truly important
in this realm.
Take caution the journey is not easy.
But once you have reaped the rewards you will
live in a world of neighborly beauty.

Carry on.

THE ONE SOUND that brings me closer to truth
finds me at the crossroads between love and d   r
destruction. I find myself visiting this place
quite often for it seems to be the only place
that makes sense. It is this ground where I find
salvation. Salvation amongst the thousands of
souls that bring life to hundreds of bodies.

And these bodies walk the earth blissfully lost
in an enchanted world of beautiful deciet.

SUNSETTING SOUL

THE SUNSET emerges an orange haze
with a purple sploch creeping through its
center.
And when my gaze is drawn downward
I find my hands buried in the sand
digging through the grains
in search of that one piece of the universe
that lifts me from the earth.

Its a connection we feel
but are slowly drawn away from as we progress.
The baby
beautiful, peaceful
no qualms, only curiousity.
Watch him move, reading the'nergies of the world.
An earthly presence with minimal reservation.

When I look into your eyes
I see all that you have seen
the uncertanties and the triumphs.
But there is nothing more beautiful
than you seeing it too.

Be my mirror
and see what I see.
A soul burning brighter than the sunset
yearning to be freed.